NUMBER FOUR
*Essays on the American West
sponsored by the
Elma Dill Russell Spencer Foundation*

How Did Davy Die?

DAVID GLENN HUNT
MEMORIAL LIBRARY
GALVESTON COLLEGE

How Did Davy Die?

By Dan Kilgore

TEXAS A&M UNIVERSITY PRESS
College Station and London

DAVID GLENN HUNT
MEMORIAL LIBRARY
GALVESTON COLLEGE

Copyright © 1978 by Dan Kilgore
All rights reserved

Library of Congress Cataloging in Publication Data

Kilgore, Daniel Edmond, 1921-
   How did Davy die?

   (Essays on the American West; no. 4)
   Includes bibliographical references.
    1. Crockett, David, 1786-1836. 2. Alamo—Siege, 1836. I. Title. II. Series.
F436.C95K54   976.4′03′0924   77-99278
ISBN 0-89096-049-6

Manufactured in the United States of America
FIRST EDITION

Acknowledgments

THIS ESSAY originated as the presidential address to the Texas State Historical Association on March 4, 1977. Many friends assisted in searching for the sources used in the original paper and in this expanded and revised version. My special thanks and gratitude go to the following people who sought out obscure references and searched for sources that never materialized: J. Richard Abell, Lucile Boykin, Doug Ferrier, Llerena Friend, Johnny and Maureen Jenkins, Chester V. Kielman and his accommodating staff at Barker Texas History Center, Christopher La Plante, Archie P. McDonald, Catherine McDowell, Malcolm D. and Margaret McLean, Robert A. Nesbitt, Rhoda Poenisch, James B. Stewart, Margaret Turner, Fred White, Sr., Dorman Winfrey, John Young, and my wife, Carol.

DAN KILGORE

How Did Davy Die?

THE GOOD LORD generously endowed David Crockett with those qualities the backwoods required: rugged strength, unusual perseverance, extraordinary courage, and fierce determination. Crockett capitalized on those gifts and employed his wit, imagination, and charm to gain national prominence as the central character of many a tall tale and to earn renown in his own time as one of America's greatest folk heroes. Yet Crockett's death at the Alamo in 1836 came as a tragic finale to a life that was essentially a failure in achievement of worldly goals. He died a poor man with an undistinguished record as a congressman.

The simplicities of backwoods life did not prepare him for the intricacies of politics in Washington. He won three congressional terms, but he failed consistently in his main political goal: to win passage of the Tennessee Vacant Land Bill. His bill would have granted frontiersmen the right to buy their homesteads at low cost and on credit. It was a bill designed for his "squatter constituency," whom he considered the nation's advance guard.

Throughout Crockett's rise to prominence as a national figure, political enemies defeated him at every turn, although both major parties used him as a symbol at various times and employed the national press to establish that symbol. During the years that Crockett supported Andrew Jackson, the Democratic press polished Crockett's image with little regard for the real man. At the same time, Whig newspapers, with just as little respect for fact, tried to laugh him out of Congress. After his opposition to Jackson's Indian Removal Bill brought about his defeat for reelection in 1831, he bitterly opposed Jackson for the rest of his life. As a result, when Crockett returned to Congress in 1833, the Democratic papers reversed their position and echoed the old Whig line against him. At that same time, the Whigs adopted and even refined the earlier image of the frontier hero started by the Democrats.

In 1835 Crockett's passionate opposition to Jackson resulted in a particularly bitter defeat for him in his try for reelection to Congress. Loss of office and of the attendant public attention cut deeply. Within weeks Crockett left Tennessee and headed for Texas.[1]

Crockett's last extant letter discloses that he and

---

[1] James Atkins Shackford, *David Crockett: The Man and the Legend* (Chapel Hill, N.C., 1956), pp. 191, 210–212, 221, 238–239, 241–245.

his party departed Tennessee in November, 1835, to explore a new country for his next move west. This was his stated purpose—and not "to fight for his rights" or even for Texas independence. He examined the country along the Red River in Texas and called it the garden spot of the world. He hoped to live there—hoped to be appointed land agent to settle the area and then to acquire the fortune that had always eluded him. When his funds ran short, he sold an engraved gold presentation watch for a cheaper timepiece and thirty dollars.

After inspecting the Red River lands, Crockett and his men made a side trip to hunt buffalo that were moving south in their annual migration.[2] By mid-January, 1836, Crockett was in San Augustine, where he signed an oath of allegiance to Texas so that he could vote and seek election to the approaching constitutional convention. He left San Augustine with the apparent intention of resuming his political career in Texas, but at that point the real David Crockett fades almost completely into myth and legend. No further written word from him survives to explain why he failed to campaign for a seat in the constitutional convention. His biographer, James Shackford, believed that Crockett's hatred for Jackson drove him instead to the Alamo.

[2] Ibid., pp. 214–216; John H. Jenkins (ed.), *The General's Tight Pants: Edward Warren's Texas Tour of 1836* (Austin, 1976).

In early 1836 two political groups and two governments, the Consultation Convention and the General Council, contended for political and military control of the budding Republic of Texas. The division, the same quarrel that drove Crockett from Tennessee, lay between pro-Jackson and anti-Jackson forces. Sam Houston, considered to be Jackson's personal representative, served as commander in chief under the Consultation Convention, but Houston could not exercise control over the command at the Alamo. Shackford believed that Crockett joined the Alamo defenders to demonstrate further opposition to the Jackson forces that had defeated him in Tennessee and not with any idea of dying for the liberty of Texas.

Crockett passed on through the capital at Washington-on-the-Brazos and entered San Antonio before February 11. He had never been known to run out on a fight, and once he arrived at the Alamo, he never left.[3] Tales of his prowess emanated from frontier observers and spread across Texas and then throughout the United States in a blend of fact and folklore.

William B. Travis mentioned in a letter dated February 25, 1836, that during the initial bombardment of the Alamo, "The Hon. David Crockett was seen at all points, animating the men to do their duty." A northern newspaper later quoted a Natchitoches man as

[3] Shackford, *David Crockett*, pp. 216–224.

saying Crockett's "unerring rifle . . . marked down" five Mexican soldiers as each stepped forward to fire a cannon planted within gunshot of the fort. A letter dated March 2 at Goliad told how Crockett probably "grinned off" the attackers. Another on March 10 said (in original spelling), "Davy Crockett and James Bowy are fighting at San Antone like tigers."[4]

After the fall of the Alamo, as a survivor of Fannin's Goliad command wrote, it was told that Crockett killed the first Mexican soldier at a distance of two hundred yards. He and Lieutenant Dickenson then allegedly burned several houses which were sheltering the enemy from Texas artillery. The same writer added, ". . . it is said and generally believed in Texas of Col. Crockett, that when Gen. Santa Anna was surveying the Alamo for the purpose of informing himself of the best method of arranging an attack, he [Crockett] made so good a shot at him as to come near taking his life, which so much enraged the General, that he resolved to storm the fort the next day and he kept his resolution."[5]

Crockett's heroism seemed to expand in direct proportion to the distance news about him had to travel. A resolution adopted after the Alamo's fall, at

[4] John H. Jenkins (ed.), *The Papers of the Texas Revolution, 1835–1836*, 10 vols. (Austin, 1973), IV, 433, 487; V, 45; *The Metropolitan* (Georgetown and Washington, D.C.), July 13, 1836.
[5] Jenkins, *Papers of the Texas Revolution*, IX, 183, 223.

a meeting in Nacogdoches on March 26, declared that "David Crockett (now rendered immortal in Glory) had fortified himself with sixteen guns well charged, and a monument of slain foes encompasses his lifeless body." A letter written from San Augustine on March 29 declared, "The Honorable David Crockett . . . was found dead with about 20 of the enemy with him and his rifle was broken to pieces it is supposed that he killed at least 20 or 30 himself."[6]

Various rumors that Crockett survived the assault on the Alamo arose almost simultaneously with his death, but no real evidence has turned up to suggest that he survived the battle. Valid documentation survives, however, to support the view that he did not fall surrounded by mounds of the slain enemy, but that he either surrendered or was captured near the end of the assault and was immediately killed by Santa Anna's order. Published references indicating that Crockett surrendered have drawn loud protests from both the press and an irate public throughout the years. Most recently *Texas Monthly* bestowed one of its 1975 uncoveted "Bum Steer" awards on what that magazine described as "A recent translation of a Mexican officer's diary which revealed that Davy Crockett surrendered at the Alamo, and was executed some time after the battle."[7]

[6] Ibid., V, 224; IX, 160.
[7] *Texas Monthly*, February, 1976, p. 79.

Lieutenant José Enrique de la Peña, who was one of Santa Anna's officers, wrote the diary during the Mexican army's Texas campaign in 1836. He did not, however, say that Crockett surrendered. Texas A&M University Press published the diary, translated from the Spanish by Carmen Perry, in October, 1975, under the title *With Santa Anna in Texas: A Personal Narrative of the Revolution*. Throughout his daily record, de la Peña was strongly critical of his general's conduct of the war against Texas. His single paragraph describing Crockett's capture and death, however, caught the eye and roused the ire of several Texas publications. Carmen Perry drew some of the barbs, although her part consisted only of rendering into English what de la Peña had written in his native language.

The diary's author participated in the storming of the Alamo on March 6, 1836, witnessed the entire battle, and recorded his observations soon afterward. His diary was first published in Mexico in 1955 in the original Spanish.

According to de la Peña, the desperate fighting ended shortly after six o'clock in the morning. Santa Anna then entered the Alamo fortifications to survey the gruesome scene and to laud his crippled battalions. De la Peña wrote:

Shortly before Santa Anna's speech, an unpleasant episode had taken place, which . . . was looked upon as base murder.

... Some seven men had survived the general carnage and, under the protection of General Castrillón, they were brought before Santa Anna. Among them ... was the naturalist David Crockett, well known in North America for his unusual adventures. ... Santa Anna answered Castrillón's intervention in Crockett's behalf with a gesture of indignation and, addressing himself to ... the troops closest to him, ordered his execution. The commanders and officers were outraged at this action and did not support the order ... ; but several officers who were around the president and who, perhaps, had not been present during the moment of danger ... thrust themselves forward, ... and with swords in hand, fell upon these unfortunate, defenseless men just as a tiger leaps upon his prey. Though tortured before they were killed, these unfortunates died without complaining and without humiliating themselves before their torturers.[8]

Six other Mexican soldiers support de la Peña's testimony that Crockett was one of several Texans who was captured or who surrendered and then was killed. Besides these seven soldiers, other sources that do not mention Crockett by name say that from five to seven Alamo defenders were taken alive, marched before Santa Anna, and executed by his order.

The most prestigious Mexican source is Ramón Martínez Caro, Santa Anna's personal secretary, who

[8] José Enrique de la Peña, *With Santa Anna in Texas: A Personal Narrative of the Revolution*, trans. and ed. Carmen Perry (College Station, Tex., 1975), pp. 52–53; J. Sanchez Garza (ed.), *La Rebelion de Texas: Manuscrito inedito de 1836, por un oficial de Santa Anna* (Mexico City, 1955), p. 70.

reported in his "True Account" that ". . . five men . . . hid themselves, and when the action was over, General Castrillón found them and brought them into the presence of Santa Anna, who, for a moment angrily reprimanded the said general, and then turned his back; at which act the soldiers already lined up, charged the prisoners and killed them."[9]

Martínez Caro's statement was largely corroborated by the first word of the fall of the Alamo delivered to General Sam Houston. On the day of the battle two ranchers living near present Floresville gathered as much information as possible from San Antonio and hurried to tell General Houston, then at Gonzales. Houston included the information in a letter written March 11 to James W. Fannin, commander at Goliad. "After the fort was carried, seven men surrendered and called for Santa Anna and quarter," Houston wrote. "They were murdered by his order."[10] Although Martínez Caro and Houston differed on the number of men involved, they agreed on basic facts.

Travelers from Texas arriving in New Orleans on March 27, 1836, three weeks after the assault, brought

[9] Carlos E. Castañeda (ed.), *The Mexican Side of the Texas Revolution* (Dallas, 1928), pp. 103–104.
[10] Jenkins, *Papers of the Texas Revolution*, V, 45–49, 52–54, 69–71; Amelia W. Williams and Eugene C. Barker (eds.), *The Writings of Sam Houston, 1813–1836*, 8 vols. (Austin, 1938), I, 362–365.

the first news of the battle. The *New Orleans Post-Union* reported that "Crockett and others had tried to surrender 'but were told there was no mercy for them.' "[11] Northern newspapers reprinted this news, which was probably the first word received throughout the United States of the fall of the Alamo and of the death of David Crockett.

Within months after the battle this account of the capture and execution of Crockett appeared in two different books published in the United States. Mary Austin Holley used the *Post-Union's* very words regarding the denial of mercy in her book *Texas*, released in July, 1836. "A desperate contest ensued," she wrote of the battle, "in which prodigies of valor were wrought by this Spartan band." She said that Crockett and six others "cried for quarter, but were told there was no mercy for them.... When their demand for quarter was refused, they continued fighting until all were butchered."[12]

The second book, also published during the summer of 1836, sought to establish a hero of gigantic proportions. Its title was *Col. Crockett's Exploits and Adventures in Texas, Written by Himself*. This apocry-

---

[11] Walter Lord, *A Time to Stand* (New York, 1961), p. 207.
[12] Mrs. Mary Austin Holley, *Texas* (Lexington, Ky., 1836), pp. 353–354; Mattie Austin Hatcher, *Letters of an Early American Traveller; Mary Austin Holley, Her Life and Works, 1784–1846* (Dallas, 1933), p. 61.

phal but best-selling "autobiography" opened the floodgates of Crockett mythology, and although patently spurious, it has remained in print in many editions through most of the years since.

While scholars have dismissed the book's version of Crockett's death as pure fiction, the "narrative" depicting the scene was largely "brought down . . . by an eye-witness," as stated on the book's title page. The lurid description of the hero's final moments, created from a montage of contemporary news clippings, primarily was extracted verbatim from the previously published statement of a Mexican prisoner who was an eyewitness.

Specific words attributed to the eyewitness appear in italics in the quotation below taken from *Exploits and Adventures*. As dawn approached, only six Alamo defenders were found alive. Crockett stood alone, a frightful gash across his forehead, in an angle of the fort, with the barrel of his shattered rifle in his right hand and with a Bowie knife, dripping blood, in his left. Some twenty dead or dying Mexicans lay around him.

[The defenders] *were instantly surrounded and ordered, by General Castrillon, to surrender,* which they did, *under a promise of his protection, finding* that *resistance any longer would be madness. . . .*

General *Castrillon was brave and not cruel, and disposed to save* the prisoners. *He marched them up to that part of the fort where stood* Santa Anna and his *murderous crew. The steady, fearless step, and undaunted tread* of Colonel Crockett in this occasion, *together with the bold demeanor* of the *hardy veteran,* had a *powerful effect* on all present. *Nothing daunted, he marched up boldly in front of Santa Anna,* and *looked him* sternly *in the face, while Castrillon addressed "his excellency,"—"Sir, here are six prisoners I have taken alive; how shall I dispose of them?" Santa Anna looked at Castrillon fiercely, flew into a violent rage, and replied, "Have I not told you before how to dispose of them? Why do you bring them to me?" At the same time his brave officers plunged their swords into the bosoms of their defenceless prisoners.*

Colonel Crockett, seeing the act of treachery, instantly sprang like a tiger at the ruffian chief, but before he could reach him a dozen swords were sheathed in his indomitable heart; and he fell, and died without a groan, a frown on his brow, and a smile of scorn and defiance on his lips. *Castrillon rushed from the scene, apparently horror-struck, sought his quarters, and did not leave them for several days, and hardly spoke to Santa Anna after.*[13]

The lines italicized above were taken from a letter written from Galveston Bay on June 9, 1836, by a correspondent of the *New York Courier and Enquirer* following an interview with an unidentified Mexican prisoner (who sounded suspiciously like Ramón Martínez Caro to historian Walter Lord) among Santa Anna's troops who had been captured at San Jacinto and who

[13] *Col. Crockett's Exploits and Adventures in Texas, Written by Himself* (Philadelphia, 1836), pp. 203–205.

were then being held on Galveston Island. After the appearance in the New York newspaper of this particular account, it was reprinted—a common journalistic practice of the time—in other publications, including the *Frankfort* (Kentucky) *Commonwealth*.[14]

More than a century later the story of Crockett's death as presented in *Exploits and Adventures* provoked what might be called the opening shot in the modern battle over the circumstances of Crockett's death. The October, 1943, issue of *Southwestern Historical Quarterly* carried a reader's inquiry about the source of a statement that Crockett "was one of the six survivors who surrendered to Santa Anna and were shot down by his orders. . . ." That statement had appeared in the *Biographical Directory of the American Congresses, 1774–1927,* and, in similar context, in the *Columbia Encyclopedia*. The editor of the quarterly did not provide an answer about the source, but he felt (as he later disclosed) that the stories of the surrender were taken from the "'spurious" ending of *Exploits and Adventures*. The editor replied simply but wrathfully,

[14] *Frankfort* (Kentucky) *Commonwealth*, July 27, 1836; Lord, *A Time to Stand,* pp. 206–207. The phrases "in an angle," "lying pell-mell," and "a frown on his brow, a smile of scorn upon his lips" appear in an article reprinted in *The Metropolitan* (Georgetown and Washington, D.C.), May 11, 1836. Andrew Briscoe reported that Crockett fell fighting "like a tiger" in the *Louisiana Advertiser*, March 28, 1836, as reprinted in the *Broome Republican* (Binghamton, N.Y.), April 21, 1836.

"The people of Tennessee and Texas will need more authority than *The Congressional Directory* and a New York publication to be convinced that David Crockett surrendered."[15] Possibly because of the editor's rebuke, both publications dropped references in later editions to the surrender.

Although sources now available do not offer absolute proof that Crockett actually surrendered or was captured, a preponderance of evidence supports the unidentified prisoner's story retold in *Exploits and Adventures*. Neither of the two known adult Texan survivors, Mrs. Dickenson and the slave Joe, saw Crockett die. Since Santa Anna and his men were the only others present, any evidence must come from them. Besides the unknown prisoner and de la Peña, four officers and a sergeant—all of whom participated in the assault and observed the final tragedy—specifically identified Crockett as one of the captives.[16] Statements from these seven Mexican soldiers were mutually corroborative and were recorded independently under

---

[15] H. Bailey Carroll, "Texas Collection," *Southwestern Historical Quarterly* 47: 178; H. Bailey Carroll, "David Crockett," in *Heroes of Texas* (Waco, 1964), p. 66; Thomas Lawrence Conelly (ed.); "Did David Crockett Surrender at the Alamo? A Contemporary Letter," *Journal of Southern History* 26: 368.

[16] Richard G. Santos, *Santa Anna's Campaign against Texas, 1835–1836: Featuring the Field Commands Issued to Major General Vicente Filisola* (Waco, 1968), pp. 76 n. 73, 84.

widely differing circumstances. Their accounts have come to light over a long period of time, several having surfaced only recently. Any one of them, standing alone, could be subject to question, but considered as a whole, the statements provide stronger documentation than can be claimed for any other incident during the battle.

The first known version by a participant to be published in permanent form appeared in the 1859 *Texas Almanac* in an article by Dr. D. N. Labadie, who had treated many wounded Mexicans after the Battle of San Jacinto. Only four or five days after Santa Anna's defeat, Dr. Labadie dressed the wounded hip of Colonel Fernando Urissa, Santa Anna's aide, who told the doctor: "I observed Castrion [*sic*] coming out of one of the quarters, leading a venerable looking old man by the hand; he [the old man] was tall, his face was red, and stooped forward as he walked." Urissa told Labadie he heard Mexicans call the man "Coket." Castrillón asked his commander to spare the "venerable old man," but Santa Anna berated him for disobeying orders to take no prisoners. Then the general ordered nearby soldiers to shoot the captive. Urissa convinced Labadie he was telling the truth about Crockett's fate.[17]

[17] James M. Day (comp.), *The Texas Almanac, 1857–1873: A Compendium of Texas History* (Waco, 1967), p. 174.

The most bizarre account of Crockett's death by a participant at the Alamo was related to Reuben M. Potter and later to John S. Ford, both important writers of Texas history. The eyewitness was Sergeant Francisco Becerra, who took upon himself a major role in the incident. Ford wrote down the sergeant's story in 1875, and it apparently appeared in print soon thereafter to stir angry criticism before fading into obscurity. In 1957 the story was extracted from Ford's manuscript memoirs and reappeared in a booklet published in Brownsville.[18] Although Sergeant Becerra is probably the least reliable Alamo eyewitness, he may be the unacknowledged source of more details written about the assault than any other participant.

After his capture at the Battle of San Jacinto, Becerra remained in Texas the rest of his life. He worked for several well-known Texans, including Mirabeau B. Lamar and Reuben M. Potter. Becerra eventually settled in Brownsville, where in 1875 Ford recorded his recollections of Santa Anna's campaign. His version of Crockett's death aroused as much indignation as did the version in de la Peña's diary published one hundred years later.

[18] José Tomás Canales (ed.), *Bits of Texas History in the Melting Pot of America: Part II, Native Latin American Contributions to Colonization and Independence of Texas* (Brownsville, 1957), pp. 19–20.

Becerra told Ford he shot the ailing Bowie in his bed after seeing Bowie kill two other Mexican soldiers with two pistols. After dispatching the Texas hero, Becerra said, he entered another room and found Travis sitting on the floor. Becerra told Ford he saw Travis offer a bugler a roll of bank bills in exchange for his life.

The bugler was dividing the money with him, Becerra said, when he saw Crockett arise from the floor where he had been lying, apparently exhausted, after the hard fight. At that moment Cos and three other generals entered the room.

As soon as Gen. Cos saw the gentleman who spoke Spanish, he rushed to him, and embraced him. He told the other generals it was Travis; that on a former occasion he had treated him like a brother, had loaned him money, etc. He also said the other man was Col. Crockett. He entreated the other generals to go with him to Gen. Santa Anna, and join with him in a request to save the lives of the two Texans. The bugler and myself followed them. They encountered the Commander-in-Chief in the court yard, with Gen. Castrillon. Gen. Cos said to him: "Mr. President, you have here two prisoners—in the name of the Republic of Mexico, I supplicate you to guarantee the lives of both." Santa Anna was very much enraged. He said: "Gentlemen generals, my order was to kill every man in the Alamo." He turned and said: "Soldiers, kill them." . . . soldiers standing around opened fire. A shot struck Travis in the back. He then stood erect, folded his arms, and looked calmly, unflinchingly, upon his assailants. He was finally killed by a ball passing through his neck. Crockett stood in a similar position. They died undaunted like heroes.[19]

Twenty years after talking with Becerra, Ford quoted him at great length on operations of the Mexican army in *Origin and Fall of the Alamo*, published in 1895. Ford chose not to use Becerra's version of Crockett's death in that work. The furor that had resulted from the earlier publication of the details apparently caused him to omit them. He wrote instead, "Sergeant Becerra was of opinion that the last two men killed were Travis and Col. Crockett, though he admitted he did not know them personally, and might be mistaken as to their identity."[20]

The appearance of the sergeant's version in print in the 1870's had drawn the fire of serious historians. In 1878 a *New York World* correspondent followed Ford's rendition of Becerra's tale closely, at times verbatim, in an article entitled "Storming of the Alamo." Although the correspondent attributed his "peculiar version of the story affecting the death of Travis and Crockett" to a soldier named "Buerra," the source certainly was Becerra.[21] The same version of the deaths

[19] Ibid; "A Mexican Sergeant's Recollections of the Alamo and San Jacinto," *Texas Mute Ranger*, April, 1882, pp. 169–172.
[20] John S. Ford, *Origin and Fall of the Alamo, March 6, 1836* (San Antonio, 1895), p. 21.
[21] *Albert Hanford's Texas State Register for 1878* (Galveston, 1878), p. 30.

of Travis and Crockett (but attributed only to "a Mexican soldier") appeared again in a historical section of an 1882 San Antonio guidebook.[22] These two publications caught the attention of historian Hubert Howe Bancroft, who denounced them. Bancroft said the stories that Travis "as well as Crockett was one of the captives put to death, are utterly unworthy of credence."[23]

Becerra's tale also eventually aroused the wrath of his former employer, historian Reuben M. Potter, who had previously praised the sergeant in his own Alamo narrative. Potter had criticized the surrender story on several other occasions through the years before encountering, in print, Becerra's version of the surrender.

In January, 1880, Potter responded to an article, "The Massacre of the Alamo," published in his hometown newspaper. He called the article a calumny against the hero and stoutly maintained that "David Crockett never surrendered to bear or tiger, Indian or Mexican."[24]

An 1883 article in the *Magazine of American History* recounting Crockett's surrender as told in *Exploits and Adventures* drew Potter's expanded criticism. Pot-

---

[22] Stephen Gould, *The Alamo City Guide, San Antonio, Texas* (San Antonio, 1882), p. 21.

[23] Hubert Howe Bancroft, *History of the North Mexican States and Texas*, 2 vols. (San Francisco, 1889), II, 211.

[24] Clipping from *The Independent Hour*, Woodbridge (?), January 26, 1880, Reuben M. Potter scrapbook, pp. 278–279, University of Texas Archives, Austin.

ter said he considered the defense of the Alamo one of the most heroic events in our history. He stated his conviction that every man in the garrison, including Crockett, fell fighting at his post—with the exception of "a few skulkers." Even these skulkers did not surrender, he said, but were dragged from their hiding place and executed.[25]

Three years later Becerra's elaborated story about Crockett's surrender appeared in the June, 1886, edition of *Magazine of American History* as "derived from a Mexican soldier in the army of Santa Anna." Potter fired off a reiteration of his position that the Alamo's defense was one of the most heroic events in history. Then he theorized, "In a fight . . . [when the hopelessly outnumbered] know they have all got to die, the bravest fall first; and the last reached is certain to be a sneak. Thus it was at the Alamo. Travis and Crockett fell early on the outworks." Potter blasted the tale attributed to the Mexican soldier: "This infamous fiction confounds [Travis and Crockett] with the group of skulkers already referred to, and ought never to have been cited, even as a rumor, in any matter which claims to be historical."[26]

[25] Marcus J. Wright, "Colonel David Crockett, of Tennessee," *Magazine of American History* 10: 489; R. M. Potter, "Colonel David Crockett," *Magazine of American History* 11: 177–178.

[26] G. Norton Galloway, "Sketch of San Antonio: The Fall of the Alamo," *Magazine of American History* 15: 532–533; R. M.

Although Becerra was not named, Potter must have known that his former servant was the source of the scorned account. Potter had used much information given him by Becerra in his study of the fall of the Alamo—an account that a serious student of the battle called the most authoritative source originating from a writer living at the time.[27] After the first publication in 1860 in pamphlet form, Potter's Alamo study gained wider circulation when reprinted in the 1868 *Texas Almanac*. Then it received national distribution in a revised and enlarged version published in the *Magazine of American History* in 1878.

Although Potter did not mention Becerra's tale of the deaths of Bowie, Travis, and Crockett in his Alamo study, he did single out the Mexican as one of "three intelligent sergeants [who provided details], who were men of fair education, and I think truthful." Potter did say that Becerra witnessed Lieutenant Dickenson's leap, saw Bowie's body on the bed, and observed the execution of the men found concealed after the battle.[28] Further, he obviously had relied heavily on Becerra's accounts of the Mexican army's march into Texas, of its

---

Potter, "The Legendary Alamo, "*Magazine of American History* 16: 211–212.

[27] Lon Tinkle, *13 Days to Glory: The Siege of the Alamo* (New York, 1958), p. 248.

[28] R. M. Potter, "The Fall of the Alamo," *Magazine of American History* 2: 19–20.

occupation of San Antonio, and of many incidents during the siege of the Alamo and the final assault.

An examination of Potter's writing shows that he changed his own position on Crockett's death. Originally he had written, "Crockett had taken refuge in a room of the lower barracks near the gate . . . he sallied to meet his fate . . . and was shot down."[29] In the 1878 revision he said, "According to Mr. Ruiz, then the Alcalde of San Antonio, who, after the action, was required to point out the slain leaders to Santa Anna, the body of Crockett was found in the west battery. . . ."[30] Furthermore, it seems apparent that initially Potter was not favorably impressed by Crockett. Potter described another Alamo hero, James Bonham, as a "polished jewel," but he referred to Crockett as a "rough gem" who represented a squatter constituency in Congress.[31] Fifty years after the battle and twenty-five years after the first publication of his study, however, Potter was quite ready to accept the heroic Crockett.

Potter's account of the defense and fall of the Alamo remained as the only major study published until the 1930's. Numerous authors of early Texas histories quoted it entirely or in part and described it as "most complete and reliable" and "most accurate."[32]

[29] Day, *Texas Almanac*, p. 257.
[30] Ibid., p. 357; Potter, "Fall of the Alamo," p. 13.
[31] Potter, "Fall of the Alamo," p. 5.
[32] John Henry Brown, *History of Texas, from 1685 to 1892,*

In 1914 Eugene C. Barker, the distinguished Texas historian, termed it the most thorough study yet made.[33] More recent works on the Alamo, supported by documents not available to Potter, prove the error of some of his conclusions, but they cannot negate his influence on earlier historians.

Nor can Potter be criticized for choosing not to use Becerra's story about the deaths of men enshrined long ago as Texas heroes, although his acceptance of Becerra's word on Mexican army activities establishes the sergeant as the principal source of many details of the siege and assault of the Alamo. When Becerra spoke on army operations, he related facts, most of which could be verified from other sources.

But Becerra's yarn about his Alamo involvement with Bowie, Travis, and Crockett was, and is, hard to believe. The truth may never be known, but the answer could lie in this forgotten man's search for personal glorification or in the telling around campfires of too many tales.

Becerra fought much longer in the service of Texas than of Mexico. According to Ford, Becerra

---

2 vols. (St. Louis, 1892), I, 569; Dudley G. Wooten (ed.), *A Comprehensive History of Texas, 1685–1897*, 2 vols. (Dallas, 1898), II, 637.

[33] Frank W. Johnson, *A History of Texas and Texans*, ed. Eugene C. Barker and E. W. Winkler, 5 vols. (Chicago, 1914), I, 410.

served in the Indian campaigns of 1839, fought in 1849 along the border under Captain Mirabeau B. Lamar, and later became "a strong supporter of the Southern cause" as a lieutenant in Captain J. F. Parker's company.[34] So much Texas military service would have pitted him against some of the world's best tall tale spinners, and all indications are that he could hold his own. Perhaps Becerra actually came to believe through years of yarn spinning that he had indeed been personally involved with the three Alamo heroes. At least he convinced Ford.

Many years passed before the appearance in print of another account of an eyewitness. In 1836 Dr. George M. Patrick had told a story involving Crockett and General Cos to W. P. Zuber, who included it long afterwards as an appendage to a letter, written in 1904, denying the surrender of any Alamo defenders. The letter was not published until 1939, when it appeared in that year's publication of the Texas Folklore Society, entitled *In the Shadow of History.*

Zuber could be called the greatest Alamo folklorist, because he is the single source for the most dramatic episodes of the gallant defense. Only through Zuber does the world know of Travis's impassioned before-the-battle speech which Zuber literally composed during "a phenomenal refreshment of memory."

[34] "A Mexican Sergeant's Recollections," p. 169.

Only on Zuber's word do we know of Travis's drawing that legendary sword-etched line in the dirt of the Alamo floor. Only Zuber told of the ailing Bowie asking his comrades to lift his cot over the line and of Moses Rose declining to step across, thereby becoming the last man to leave the garrison and escape the slaughter.

Many historians have questioned Zuber's tales, and some have voiced doubt that Rose was ever a member of the Alamo garrison. Zuber devoted much of his later life to writing down, then defending, what his parents had gleaned from Moses Rose while Rose recuperated at the Zuber home during his 1836 flight from the Alamo. Appropriately, Zuber's 1904 letter appeared in the same publication that first offered proof, from testimony entered in the early records of Nacogdoches County, that Rose had been present at the Alamo.

The primary thrust of Zuber's letter published by the Texas Folklore Society was that the tales of the Texans found in hiding after the battle were nothing more than fabrications. After discounting these stories, Zuber recounted what Dr. George M. Patrick told him about the capture of Crockett.

According to Zuber, Dr. Patrick said that he visited General Martín Perfecto de Cos, Santa Anna's brother-in-law, while Cos was being held prisoner after his capture at San Jacinto. Patrick asked the general if he had seen Crockett and if he knew how he had died. Cos answered that he, not Castrillón, had found Crockett, who was well dressed and locked alone in a room in the barracks. Zuber then composed a fanciful entreaty by Crockett, presumably based on what he said Patrick had told him years earlier. Zuber quoted Crockett as explaining that he came to Texas to explore and to become a loyal Mexican citizen, and that he had done no fighting. Following this, Zuber presented a similarly flowery plea by Cos, who had taken Crockett before Santa Anna with the supplication that his brother-in-law spare the distinguished former congressman. Zuber had Santa Anna answering impatiently, "You know your orders," and turning away. Crockett struck at Santa Anna with a dagger, but "was met by a bayonet-thrust by the hand of a soldier through the heart."

Zuber denounced this tale as a gross falsehood because of inaccurate details, which he had provided himself. Yet when he later wrote his memoirs, he gave differing versions of these same details. It appears that Zuber, as he once accused a historian who questioned him, ". . . sometimes relied too much upon his memory in stating historical facts."

Zuber began and ended his letter by stating that not one Texan "escaped or surrendered, or tried to do so; but every man of them died fighting." To admit that any of the brave defenders, particularly Crockett, surrendered or were captured would violate Zuber's basic theme of the Alamo defense as a great heroic epic. Still, Zuber's letter documented a significant fact: General Cos told Dr. Patrick that Crockett was captured and then executed. When considered with statements of the other eyewitnesses, the letter provides additional evidence that Crockett did survive the fighting.[35]

Until 1955, however, available sources really afforded little reason for historians to believe that Crockett was murdered by Santa Anna's order. The early accounts by Urissa and Becerra have a ring of folklore instead of history, and Zuber's letter mentioning General Cos certainly lends no credence to the story. But in 1955 came the publication in Mexico, in original Spanish, of Lieutenant Colonel de la Peña's diary. In the years following, additional documentation appeared. Besides de la Peña's translated narrative, two other valid eyewitness account have been published in

[35] W. P. Zuber to Charlie Jeffries, "Inventing Stories about the Alamo," in *In the Shadow of History* (Austin, 1939), pp. 42–47; W. P. Zuber, "Eighty Years in Texas: Reminiscences of a Texas Veteran from 1830 to 1910" (manuscript), pp. 208–214, Texas State Archives, Austin; W. P. Zuber, "The Escape of Rose from the Alamo," *The Quarterly of the Texas State Historical Association*, 5: 5; 6: 68; R. B. Blake, "A Vindication of Rose and His Story," in *In the Shadow of History*, pp. 29–34.

the United States since 1960. These accounts, in addition to the basic facts of Crockett's death as told in *Exploits and Adventures* and now known to be based on a participant's recollections, create a massive body of evidence.

An eyewitness account of another San Jacinto prisoner of war (a high-ranking but unknown officer), appeared in the August, 1960, issue of the *Journal of Southern History*. The account was originally published in the *Detroit Democratic Free Press* of September 7, 1836.

George M. Dolson, a sergeant in the Texas army, included the account in a letter written to his brother in Detroit on July 19, 1836, only a few months after Santa Anna's defeat at San Jacinto. On the day before, Dolson had interpreted a statement made by a Mexican officer, unfortunately unidentified, describing Crockett's death.

The officer was quoted as saying, "... on the morning the Alamo was captured, between the hours of five and six o'clock, General Castrillon, who fell at the battle of San Jacinto, entered the back room of the Alamo, and there found Crockett and five other Americans, who had defended it until defence was useless." Castrillón restrained his soldiers and marched the captives before Santa Anna after promising to save them.

Dolson continued the officer's account: "Colonel

Crockett was in the rear, had his arms folded, and appeared bold as the lion as he passed my informant. Almonte, Santa Anna's interpreter, knew Colonel Crockett, and said to my informant, 'the one behind is the famous Crockett.'" Santa Anna reprimanded Castrillón and commanded his soldiers to shoot the prisoners.

The officer's straightforward statement provides details found in no other source. Significantly, he was not quoted as saying that Crockett or the others had surrendered.[36]

The second source to appear in print in the 1960's was not so lengthy or so clear as Dolson's letter. It is part of the evidence, however, and should be included

[36] Conelly, "Did David Crockett Surrender at the Alamo?" pp. 368–376. Dolson's informant has been erroneously identified as Juan Nepomuceno Almonte because one sentence of the letter has been garbled in transcription. As given, it reads,". . . appeared bold as the lion as he passed my informant (Almonte). Santa Anna's interpreter knew Colonel Crockett. . . ." This rendering does not make sense, and the passage should read, ". . . appeared bold as the lion as he passed my informant. Almonte, Santa Anna's interpreter, knew Colonel Crockett. . . ." Almonte was educated in the United States and certainly would not have had a man only a few months in Texas translate for him. He was, in fact, Santa Anna's interpreter and not only interpreted for him with General Houston after San Jacinto but also later accompanied his chief to Washington as aide and interpreter. See "Juan Nepomuceno Almonte," in *The Handbook of Texas*, ed. Walter Prescott Webb, 2 vols. (Austin, 1952), I, 35; and Ann Fears Crawford (ed.), *The Eagle: The Autobiography of Santa Anna* (Austin, 1967), pp. 55–57.

with the other eyewitness accounts. A brief statement about Crockett's death is included in the translated excerpts from the memoirs of Lieutenant Colonel José Juan Sánchez Navarro which were published in Mexico in 1966 and in the United States in 1968.

Sánchez Navarro, who led the assault on the Alamo at the head of the first column under General Cos, wrote, "By six-thirty in the morning not a single enemy existed. . . . Some cruelties horrified me, among them the death of an oldster (*anciano*) whom they called Cocran. . . ."

Sánchez Navarro did not know English, and he could easily have mistaken "Crockett" for "Cocran." A Robert Cochran was indeed an Alamo defender, but Crockett, at age fifty, would better fit the description of *anciano* than the twenty-six-year-old Cochran. In 1836 many men were old at fifty years. Furthermore, Colonel Urissa also referred to Crockett as an old man. Fatigue from the stress of battle could have given him the appearance of age far beyond his fifty years.[37]

Although the eyewitnesses agree that Santa Anna

---

[37] Miguel A. Sanchez Lamego, *The Siege and Taking of the Alamo*, trans. Consuelo Velasco (Santa Fe, 1968), p. 37; Carlos Sanchez Navarro, *La Guerra de Tejas: Memorias de un soldado* (Mexico, 1960), p. 84; Amelia Williams, "A Critical Study of the Siege of the Alamo and of the Personnel of Its Defenders," *Southwestern Historical Quarterly* 37: 252.

uttered the fatal order for the execution of the Texans, none of the general's personal writings even hint at the incident. But Santa Anna would have sought, of course, to avoid mentioning that it ever occurred. In his official report dictated at eight o'clock that morning, the general said he had viewed the corpses of Travis, Bowie, and Crockett, but he added nothing more. Santa Anna devoted only one paragraph of his autobiography to the assault on the Alamo and pointedly said, ". . . not one soldier showed signs of desiring to surrender, and with fierceness and valor, they died fighting." All indications are that he tried to absolve himself of any blame for the heartless executions.[38]

Not one report of an eyewitness has been found by Alamo scholars to support the popular notion that Crockett went down while desperately clubbing Mexican soldiers with the barrel of his shattered rifle. Nonetheless, most historians have concluded from statements made by two known "Texian" survivors of the battle (neither of whom witnessed the event) that he died fighting.

Mrs. Almeron Dickenson, widowed during the attack, lay in hiding clutching her infant daughter while the fighting raged. She gave her version of the

---

[38] Day, *Texas Almanac*, pp. 611–613; Crawford, *The Eagle*, p. 51.

battle numerous times throughout the years. The other survivor, who has lived through history simply as "Joe," was the twenty-one-year-old slave of Colonel Travis. Joe also remained hidden during the fighting. Later he accompanied the grieving Mrs. Dickenson and her baby to bear the tragic news to the Texas army as it fell back before the advancing Mexicans.

Both Mrs. Dickenson and Joe assumed that Crockett died in hand-to-hand combat. They related almost identical stories. Both told of being discovered in their hiding places by an English-speaking officer. Each suffered slight wounds during capture. Both witnessed the killing of a Texas gunner named Walker. Mexican soldiers must have found both at about the same time and place, near the end of the bloodiest fighting.

Even their earliest recorded statements reflected heavy editorial assistance aimed at building the Crockett legend. The *Telegraph and Texas Register* of March 24, 1836, reported Mrs. Dickenson as saying, "The end of David Crockett of Tennessee, the great hunter of the west, was as glorious as his career . . . had been useful. He and his companions were found surrounded by piles of assailants, whom they had immolated on the altar of Texas liberties." In a later interview she was quoted as saying, "I recognized Col. Crockett lying dead and mutilated between the church and two story barrack building, and even remember seeing his peculiar cap lying by his side."[39] Joe appeared before cabinet members of the infant Republic of Texas on March 20, 1836, and a northern newspaper quoted him: "Crockett, the kind hearted, brave David Crockett, and a few of the devoted friends who entered the Fort with him, were found lying together, with 24 of the slain enemy around him."[40]

Whatever the two survivors observed while being escorted through Santa Anna's milling troops would have been seen under intense stress and even in the shadow of imminent death. Both said simply that they saw the bodies of Crockett and several others lying in the open yard. Both described the scene as it would appear if Crockett and others had been brought before Santa Anna and executed.

The facts related by Mrs. Dickenson and Joe, then, can be considered actually to lend additional support to the version told by the Mexican soldiers. Mrs. Dickenson's statement that she saw Crockett's body "mutilated" adds further substance. Since both passed through the Alamo yard just as the battle ended, and neither saw Crockett alive, their stories indicate that

[39] J. M. Morphis, *History of Texas* (New York, 1875), p. 177.

[40] *Harrisburg* (Pennsylvania) *Reporter and State Journal*, May 20, 1836. The report must have been written by William F. Gray, for it is given verbatim in his *From Virginia to Texas, 1835* (1965 reprint; Houston, 1909), pp. 136–138.

the Texas soldiers must have been executed immediately after their capture.

As for the stories of Crockett turning up alive after the Alamo's fall, most may be dismissed immediately. One tale with apparent documentation continues to surface occasionally and is often confused with eyewitness accounts. The documentation consists of several 1840 newspaper articles.

The story originated with a letter written by a "William C. White" and printed in the *Austin City Gazette* of March 18, 1840. White, who said he lived in Mexico, wrote of a visit to Guadalajara, where a Mexican told him about a Texas prisoner forced to work in a mine. According to White, the prisoner was none other than Crockett, who had been taken alive and sent to Mexico. White said he visited Crockett, who wrote a letter to his family in Tennessee and asked White to mail it for him. White wrote that he mailed the letter in Matamoros and later gave a copy to David L. Wood, a filibuster then serving with Mexican federalists of the Republic of the Rio Grande.

The *City Gazette* editor published White's letter, but expressed his suspicions about its reliability. In the April 1, 1840, issue, that same editor exposed a hoax. He had proved the letter from "William C. White" to be in the handwriting of David L. Wood.

The story spread much faster than its refutation.

Niles' National Register reprinted "White's" letter on April 25, 1840, but did not reveal it as a fraud until June 6. Meanwhile, the news naturally aroused the hopes of John Crockett, David's son, who was then a congressman from Tennessee. The Crockett family had never received the letter supposedly mailed from Matamoros, but John Crockett wanted more details. He sent the U.S. secretary of state a request (dated April 30) that the minister to Mexico investigate the report. John Crockett wrote, "While Santa Anna was a prisoner in Texas, I am informed, he stated to a number of gentlemen, that he [Crockett] was saved alive by Alcuante [*sic*], and that he, Santa Anna, ordered him put to death after it was all over."[41] The false letter apparently raised John Crockett's hopes to the extent that he started for Mexico in search of his father.[42]

Wood's motives in fabricating the hoax are not clear. He arrived in Texas in early 1839 armed with a letter to Mirabeau B. Lamar from the Illinois secretary of state, who praised Wood's ability as a young editor and as a naturalist of "the first Respectability." Wood soon began publishing the "first literary paper in Texas," the *Richmond Telescope and Texas Literary Mes-*

[41] Frederick C. Chabot (ed.) *Texas Letters*, Yanaguana Society Publications, Vol. 5 (San Antonio, 1940), pp. 73–74.

[42] Ibid., pp. 73–75; John H. Jenkins (ed.), "Did Davy Crockett Survive the Alamo?" *Texana* 1: 284–288; Shackford, *David Crockett*, p. 239; Conelly, "Did David Crockett Surrender?" p. 371.

senger, in which he aspired to combine "literary and scientific matter" with "general subjects . . . of interest and utility." Apparently he edited the paper for only a few weeks before resigning because his associate in the venture wished to "promulgate political principles repugnant" to Wood's feelings. Some time later a grand jury indicted Wood for the crime of miscegenation. He might have gone to Mexico in the cause of liberty, to live in peace with his true love, or to avoid prosecution. Whatever provoked him to fabricate the strange tale about Crockett in Mexico is open to even greater speculation.[43]

Wood's hoax, nevertheless, was more believable than the flood of Davy Crockett myths and legends that began to circulate after the Alamo's fall. The folk character that Crockett himself had nurtured assumed truly heroic proportions with his death, largely through the torrent of Crockett almanacs that recounted his mythical and often superhuman adventures. Beginning with the first one in 1835, while Crockett was yet alive, the almanacs steadily issued forth until at least fifty had appeared before the publication of the final one in 1856.[44] In more recent years the legendary Davy has

[43] Charles Adam Gulick, Jr., et al. (eds.), *The Papers of Mirabeau Buonaparte Lamar*, 6 vols. (Austin, 1920–1927), V, 244, 271, 280–281, 291; Harold Schoen, "The Free Negro in the Republic of Texas," *Southwestern Historical Quarterly* 40: 170.

[44] Constance Rourke, *Davy Crockett* (1962 reprint; New

been reincarnated by John Wayne in the motion picture *The Alamo* and by Fess Parker in the Walt Disney television series.

With all this fervent publicity that has elevated Crockett to the "King of Wild Frontier," it is little wonder that serious historians have not emphasized the circumstances of the hero's death. Authors of most major works on Texas history seem to agree that Santa Anna's soldiers captured and later executed several Texans at the Alamo, but few include Crockett among them. The majority of the authors devote little space to his death—if they mention it at all. The most common reference made is a simple statement that Crockett's body was found surrounded by bodies of the fallen enemy. Mrs. Anna Pennybacker, the ultimate authority for generations of earlier Texans, added a flourish in the first edition of her *A New History of Texas for Schools*. She wrote, "Brave Crockett left a score of bodies about him to show his work."[45] In some later revisions, however, she dropped any mention of his death.

A primary reason for the brevity regarding Crockett's role at the Alamo is that surprisingly few thorough

---

York, 1934), pp. 234–237. A writer in one of the almanacs described how Crockett feigned death during the battle and then later avenged his executed comrades by killing their slayers with his hunting knife (ibid., p. 217).

[45] Anna J. Hardwicke Pennybacker, *A New History of Texas for Schools* (Tyler, 1888), p. 78.

studies have been made about the Alamo's defense and fall. Almost a century elapsed after the battle before Amelia Williams compiled her massive *A Critical Study of the Siege of the Alamo.* She assumed from Mrs. Dickenson's account that Crockett fell while fighting not far from the church.[46] Lon Tinkle, in *13 Days to Glory,* also followed Mrs. Dickenson, but he expressed doubt that any Texans were captured. He classed the story that Crockett surrendered along with those legends about the escape of Crockett.[47]

At least two other contemporary authors have examined the now-available Mexican sources and say that Crockett might indeed have been taken, then killed. Walter Lord, whose diligent research and careful appraisal of original sources make his *A Time to Stand* the best recent study of the Alamo, mentions that two of the most reliable eyewitnesses said Crockett was one of the murdered captives. In an epilogue entitled "Riddles of the Alamo," Lord discusses the various eyewitness accounts and concludes that it is indeed possible that Crockett surrendered.[48] The second contemporary author, Richard G. Santos, who wrote *Santa Anna's Campaign against Texas, 1835–1836,* based in part on the general's order book of field commands, points out

[46] Amelia Williams, "A Critical Study of the Siege of the Alamo," p. 43.
[47] Tinkle, *13 Days to Glory,* pp. 221, 224.
[48] Lord, *A Time to Stand,* pp. 175, 206.

that four of Santa Anna's men identified Crockett as one of the unfortunates killed after the battle.[49]

Little doubt now remains that Mexican troops captured several Texans in the final moments of the storming of the Alamo. Statements from seven of Santa Anna's men who were present as eyewitnesses say specifically that David Crockett was one of those taken alive. A reconstruction of the final drama thus can be drawn from the accounts of those who observed it.

As the assault waned about six o'clock that morning of March 6, 1836, General Castrillón found Crockett and several others and marched them into the open Alamo yard. (It deserves repeating here that the most creditable of the eyewitnesses did not say the Texans surrendered.) Santa Anna had entered the blood-soaked grounds to address his assembling troops, and his reply to Castrillón's plea for mercy for the surviving Texans was immediate and terribly final. Soldiers still in the grip of battle fever sprang to execute his order of death. The evidence suggests that the entire episode— from the discovery of the Texans until their deaths— took place within only a few minutes.

The author of what has become known as the definitive biography of Crockett, James Shackford, did not have access to the best of these eyewitness accounts.

---

[49] Santos, *Santa Anna's Campaign against Texas*, pp. 76 n. 73, 84.

Shackford accepted the story of an alleged Alamo survivor, Madam Candelaria, although he admitted that no one will ever know whether she was actually present inside the Alamo. He simply wrote, "David's death was quite undramatic . . . he was one of the first to fall . . . and he died unarmed."[50]

Shackford's interests rightfully lay more in the man than in the legends, and in summing up Crockett's death, he composed this moving epitaph:

> Too much has been made over the details of *how* David died at the Alamo. Such details are not important. What is important is that he died as he had lived. His life was one of indomitable bravery; his death was a death of intrepid courage. His life was one of wholehearted dedication to his concepts of liberty. He died staking his life against what he regarded as intolerable tyranny. A poor man who had long known the devastating consequences of poverty and who all his life had fought a dedicated fight for the right of the dispossessed to a new opportunity, he died defending a poor and insecure people and proclaiming their rights to participate in the arts of self-government. . . . This is the true significance of the death and rebirth of David Crockett.[51]

[50] Shackford, *David Crockett*, pp. 229, 234.
[51] Ibid., pp. 238–239.

DAVID GLENN HUNT
MEMORIAL LIBRARY
GALVESTON COLLEGE